MW00889209

"If anyone loves Me, he will
keep My word; and My Father
will love him, and We will come
to him and make Our abode
with him."

~John 14:23

THIS JOURNAL BELONGS

TO

"Blessed are those who mourn, for they shall be comforted."
~Matthew 5:4

"You are My friends if you do what I command you."
~John 15:14

"Blessed are the merciful, for they shall receive mercy."
~Matthew 5:7

"But if you do not forgive others, then your Father
will not forgive your transgressions."
~Matthew 6:15

"Blessed are the pure in heart, for they shall see God."
~Matthew 5:8

"If you abide in Me, and My words abide in you,
ask whatever you wish, and it will be done for you."
~John 15:7

... keep your tongue from evil and your lips from telling lies.

Psalm 34:13

"Blessed are the peacemakers, for they shall be called sons of God."
~Matthew 5:9

"I am the vine, you are the branches; he who abides in Me and I in him, he bears much fruit, for apart from Me you can do nothing ."
~John 15:5

*"Blessed are those who have been persecuted
for the sake of righteousness, for theirs is the kingdom of heaven."*
~Matthew 5:10

"Greater love has no one than this,
that one lay down his life for his friends."
~John 15:13

"Do not judge so that you will not be judged."
~Matthew 7:1

*"If I had not come and spoken to them, they would not have sin,
but now they have no excuse for their sin."*
~Matthew 15:22

"This is My commandment, that you love one another,
just as I have loved you."
~John 15:12

"If anyone wants to sue you and take your shirt, let him have your coat also."
~Matthew 5:40

"Enter through the narrow gate; for the gate is wide and the way is broad that leads to destruction, and there are many who enter through it."
~Matthew 7:13

"But I say to you, do not resist an evil person;
but whoever slaps you on your right cheek, turn the other to him also."
~Matthew 5:39

"For the gate is small and the way is narrow that leads to life, and there are few who find it."
~Matthew 7:14

"Behold, I have given you authority to tread on serpents and scorpions,
and over all the power of the enemy, and nothing will injure you."
~Luke 10:19

"Beware of the false prophets, who come to you in sheep's clothing,
but inwardly are ravenous wolves."
~Matthew 7:15

"For the Son of Man has come to seek and to save that which was lost."
~Luke 19:10

"Give to him who asks of you,
and do not turn away from him who wants to borrow from you."
~Matthew 5:42

"In the same way, I tell you, there is joy in the presence of the angels of God
over one sinner who repents."
~Luke 15:10

"But I say to you, love your enemies and pray for those who persecute you."
~Matthew 5:44

"So that you may be sons of your Father who is in heaven; for He causes His sun to rise on the evil and the good, and sends rain on the righteous and the unrighteous."
~Matthew 5:45

*"Truly I say to you, whoever does not receive
the kingdom of God like a child will not enter it at all."*
~Luke 18:17

"Yet not a hair of your head will perish.
By your endurance you will gain your lives."
~Luke 21:18-19

"But blessed are your eyes, because they see;
and your ears, because they hear."
~Matthew 13:16

"And the one on whom seed was sown on the good soil, this is the man
who hears the word and understands it; who indeed bears fruit and brings forth,
some a hundredfold, some sixty, and some thirty."
~Matthew 13:23

"But you, when you pray, go into your inner room,
close your door and pray to your Father who is in secret,
and your Father who sees what is done in secret will reward you."
~Matthew 6:6

*"Truly, truly, I say to you, an hour is coming and now is,
when the dead will hear the voice of the Son of God,
and those who hear will live."*
~John 5:25

"Bless those who curse you, pray for those who mistreat you."
~Luke 6:28

"See that you do not despise one of these little ones,
for I say to you that their angels in heaven
continually   see the face of My Father who is in heaven."
~Matthew 18:10

"He who is not with Me is against Me;
and he who does not gather with Me, scatters."
~Luke 11:23

And looking at them Jesus said to them,
"With people this is impossible, but with God all things are possible."
~Matthew 19:26

"He who eats My flesh and drinks My blood has eternal life, and I will raise him up on the last day."
~John 6:54

And He summoned the crowd with His disciples, and said to them,
"If anyone wishes to come after Me, he must deny himself,
and take up his cross and follow Me."
~Mark 8:34

"Just as the Son of Man did not come to be served,
but to serve, and to give His life a ransom for many."
~Matthew 20:28

"For what does it profit a man to gain the whole world,
and forfeit his soul?"
~Mark 8:36

"And he who falls on this stone will be broken to pieces;
but on whomever it falls, it will scatter him like dust."
~Matthew 21:44

"For what will a man give in exchange for his soul?"
~Mark 8:37

He said to him, "You shall love the Lord, your God, with all your heart,
with all your soul, and with all your mind"
~Matthew 22:37

"Therefore I say to you, all things for which you pray and ask, believe that you have received them, and they will be granted you."
~Mark 11:24

"Whoever exalts himself will be humbled;
but whoever humbles himself will be exalted."
~Matthew 23:12

_____

_____

_____

_____

_____

_____

_____

_____

_____

_____

_____

_____

_____

_____

_____

_____

_____

_____

_____

_____

_____

_____

_____

"Whenever you stand praying, forgive, if you have anything against anyone, so that your Father who is in heaven will also forgive you your transgressions."
~Mark 11:25

"*For many will come in My name, saying, 'I am the Christ,' and will mislead many.*"
~Matthew 24:5

_____

_____

_____

_____

_____

_____

_____

_____

_____

_____

_____

_____

_____

_____

_____

_____

_____

_____

_____

_____

———⬥❖⬥———

"These things I have spoken to you, so that in Me you may have peace. In the world you have tribulation, but take courage; I have overcome the world."
~John 16:33

So Jesus said to Peter, "Put the sword into the sheath;
the cup which the Father has given Me, shall I not drink it?"
~John 18:11

"Blessed is that slave whom his master finds so doing when he comes."
~Matthew 24:46

———❧———

" For this reason I say to you, do not be worried about your life, as to what you will eat or
what you will drink; nor for your body, as to what you will put on. Is not life more than food,
and the body more than clothing?"
~Matthew 6:25

"Keep watching and praying that you may not enter into temptation;
the spirit is willing, but the flesh is weak."
~Matthew 26:41

"Look at the birds of the air, that they do not sow,
nor reap nor gather into barns, and yet your heavenly Father feeds them.
Are you not worth much more than they?"
~Matthew 6:26

"And who of you by being worried can add a single hour to his life? "
~Matthew 6:27

"For whoever does the will of God, he is My brother and sister and mother."
~Mark 3:35

"But if God so clothes the grass of the field, which is alive today and tomorrow is thrown into the furnace, will He not much more clothe you? You of little faith!"
~Matthew 6:30

"For from within, out of the heart of men, proceed the evil thoughts, fornications, thefts, murders, adulteries, deeds of coveting and wickedness, as well as deceit, sensuality, envy, slander, pride and foolishness."
~Mark 7:21-22

"For whoever gives you a cup of water to drink because of your name
as followers of Christ, truly I say to you, he will not lose his reward."
~Mark 9:41

"But seek first His kingdom and His righteousness, and all these things will be added to you."
~Matthew 6:33

"So do not worry about tomorrow; for tomorrow will care for itself.
Each day has enough trouble of its own."
~ Matthew 6:34

_____
_____
_____
_____
_____
_____
_____
_____
_____
_____
_____
_____
_____
_____
_____
_____
_____
_____
_____
_____

"Ask, and it will be given to you; seek, and you will find; knock, and it will be opened to you."
~Matthew 7:7

"Or what man is there among you who,
when his son asks for a loaf, will give him a stone?"
~Matthew 7:9

"Either make the tree good and its fruit good, or make the tree bad and its fruit bad; for the tree is known by its fruit."
~Matthew 12:33

"For what will a man give in exchange for his soul?"
~Mark 8:37

Jesus said to them, "It is not those who are healthy who need a physician, but those who are sick; I did not come to call the righteous, but sinners."
~Mark 2:17

"The eye is the lamp of the body; so then if your eye is clear,
your whole body will be full of light."
~ Matthew 6:22

"For truly I say to you, if you have faith the size of a mustard seed, you will say to this mountain, 'Move from here to there,' and it will move; and nothing will be impossible to you."
~Matthew 17:20

"And all things you ask in prayer, believing, you will receive."
~Matthew 21:22

"For by your words you will be justified, and by your words you will be condemned."
~Matthew 12:37

"Come to Me, all who are weary and heavy-laden, and I will give you rest."
~Matthew 11:28

"Take My yoke upon you and learn from Me, for I am gentle and humble in heart, and you will find rest for your souls."
~Matthew 11:29

So Jesus said to them, "Truly, truly, I say to you, unless you eat the flesh of the Son of Man and drink His blood, you have no life in yourselves."
~John 6:53

"Truly I say to you, unless you are converted and become like children,
you will not enter the kingdom of heaven."
~Matthew 18:3

_"Truly I say to you, among those born of women
there has not arisen anyone greater than John the Baptist!
Yet the one who is least in the kingdom of heaven is greater than he."_
~Matthew 11:11

_____

_____

_____

_____

_____

_____

_____

_____

_____

_____

_____

_____

_____

_____

_____

_____

_____

_____

_____

_____

_____

*"Truly, truly, I say to you, an hour is coming and now is,
when the dead will hear the voice of the Son of God, and those who hear will live."*
~John 5:25

"For My yoke is easy and My burden is light."
~Matthew 11:30

Made in the USA
Lexington, KY
31 January 2018